WELCOME AND ENJOY!

Aït Benhaddou, Morocco

Chicago, USA

Cinque Terre, Italy

Dubrovnik, Croatia

Hassan Tower, Rabat, Morocco

Gamcheon Culture Village, Busan, Korea

Eltz Castle, Wierschem, Germany

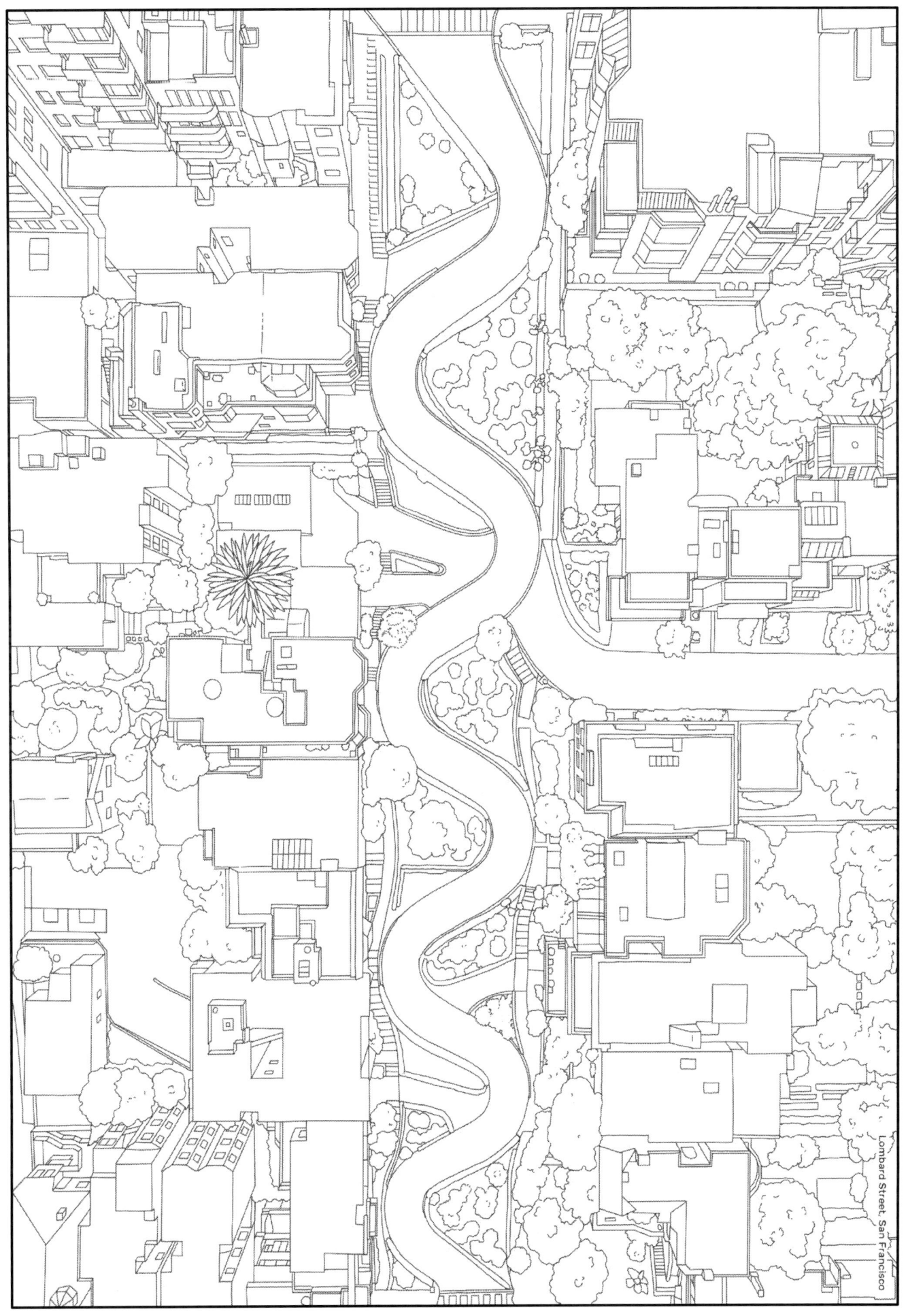

Lombard Street, San Francisco

Santorini, Greece

Fez, Morocco

Tian-Yuan Temple, Taiwan

Porto, Portugal

Vatican, Italy

Rotterdam, Netherlands

Ronda, Spain

www.bookoloring.com

"ICONIC PLACES : A COLORING BOOK FOR ADULTS"

COPYRIGHT © 2020 BOOKOLORING.COM
ALL RIGHTS RESERVED.
NO PART OF THIS PUBLICATION MAY BE REPRODUCED,
DISTRIBUTED, OR TRANSMITTED IN ANY FORM OR BY ANY MEANS,
INCLUDING PHOTOCOPYING, RECORDING, OR OTHERS ELECTRONICS
OR MECHANICALS METHODS.

DESIGN AND ILLUSTRATION BY CAMILA NOGUEIRA
CAMILA_ILLUSTRATION

Made in the USA
Monee, IL
24 January 2021